# THE
# UNDERDOG

*Achieving Your Dreams Against the Odds*

MARK LLEWHELLIN

Book 1 in the
Mark Llewhellin
Success and Happiness Series

# DEDICATION

This book is dedicated to someone who means more to me than anything I can ever do, achieve, or become: My little miracle – Léon James Llewhellin.

This book is also dedicated to you and every Underdog out there who has had people doubt them or say, "You won't do it" or "It can't be done.

# TABLE OF CONTENTS

# INTRODUCTION

So here we go with my first book. Like many things in my life, I consider it a miracle that I've written a book. When I was younger, I never thought I'd amount to anything, I wasn't the most popular kid, I wasn't the one that all the girls chased, I wasn't the brightest kid in the class, and I wasn't the athletics superstar. In fact, running the school cross country course, which was less than 2 miles, was too much for me without stopping.

When it came to athletics and cross country, I would do my best to avoid it. It wasn't that I disliked running, I hated it, and I mean hate with a passion! You'll often read in self-development books that you have to follow your passion to do well and achieve on a high level. But if there was one thing I hated with a passion, it was running.

But like many kids I had a dream, a dream that I would one day become somebody special, that one day I would achieve things that many would consider impossible.

Have you ever had a dream or a goal that you wanted to achieve and found out that there are people (yes, even friends and family) who think you've got no chance and you're stupid for thinking you want to achieve something so big?

The truth is that most people underestimate what they can achieve, they underestimate the power of the mind, and they underestimate what they can achieve when they put their minds to it.

This can limit their belief in themselves and can ultimately stop them achieving great things in their lives. So belief is important to success, but if you're anything like me or what I was like, you may not 100% believe in yourself. That's OK: all you need to do is think it's possible.

When I was thinking about what I should call this book, I thought about my life and how things have turned out for me.

There are some bits about my life which I will mention in this book, but the purpose of this book isn't to be an autobiography, but to help you on your path to achieving what you want out of your own life.

I believe that no matter what your race, gender, religion, sexuality or age, there will be something in this book for you.

As you go through this book, you will see that some of the writing is in a bold format. The reason I have done this is because I'd like you to take special note of these words.

I've read many books on self-development and they have changed my life beyond recognition.

If you want more out of life and want to live the very best life you can, not only for yourself but also for your friends and family, then read on.

What this book will hopefully give you is belief: belief in yourself to know that you can achieve big things in your life and that you can make a difference in the lives of others.

If I can achieve what was once considered impossible for me, then hopefully you'll think, "If he can do that from where he started, then I've got a chance of making my own dreams come true."

Sometimes we look at people who have achieved impressive things and we think that's just the way they are and it's probably the way they've always been. But the truth is, most of the high achievers we read or hear about have at one stage also been underdogs. They have had to battle through challenges and by applying certain principles to their life they have triumphed against the odds and achieved their dreams.

In this book I am going to be very transparent, I'll let you take a little peak into my life and hopefully you'll get one or two useful pieces of information that will help you on your journey. Sometimes people may look at me and think I never have a challenging day, maybe I brush things off easily and simply float through life. There is some truth in that and over the years I have learned certain things that have helped me to handle challenges a bit better than most people, but like you, I am still human. I have emotions, feelings and sometimes, yes, even negative thoughts. However, there are ways to bounce back quicker from setbacks, and in this book you will read about some of the techniques I have used to take me from failure to success.

There are those people who will want to tear you down and can be pretty insulting at times. Over the years, I've been referred to in various negative ways: the wrong skin colour, fat, physically unfit, mumbles (some of the children in school used to call me this as I didn't speak very clearly at times), ugly, bald, ginger (my beard), too old and too young. I've had a lot more insults than this, but I thought I'd just tell you about the kind ones.

As with the running, I can honestly say that I didn't have an initial passion for physically writing a book. Oh, sure, like many people, I want a book out, but put the work in to make it a reality... HELL NO! It takes time to write a book, and it means I have to sit down and write, which isn't my idea of fun.

In fact, I'd rather be doing what I really love, which is sitting in front of the TV and eating Ben and Jerry's Chocolate Fudge Brownie ice cream all day long. Mmmmmmmmmmmm chocolate fudge brownie with hot chocolate fudge cake. My idea of heaven is eating piles of junk food, achieving loads, and having the same body that Jean-Claude Van Damme had in "Blood Sport."

I know, I know... I'm supposed to be this health and fitness expert who doesn't eat any crap and wakes up shouting "hallelujah" every morning, but it's not quite like that. I have flaws and faults, and I'm far from perfect.

When it came to producing this book, I had no ghost writer, no massive publishing house behind me and no huge marketing campaign, but I did have a dream to get a book published. Writing this book has been a similar process to when I first started running at the age of 16. I tripped, I fell back, I missed deadlines, I had setbacks and I temporarily I failed but I never gave up.

My hope for you is that you'll get something of use out of this book that can help you to achieve your dreams in life.

You may or may not know me personally, but we do have one thing in common: at some point in our lives we've been able to say... "We are The Underdogs."

# CHAPTER 1

# YOU ARE A MIRACLE –
# LIFE IS A MIRACLE

*"There are only two ways to live your life. One is as though nothing is a miracle. The other is as though everything is a miracle."*
– Albert Einstein

The Underdog

You are a walking, breathing miracle. While we are on the path to achieving our dreams and goals, it's very easy to forget how amazing we really are. We get caught up in negative thoughts: "I'm not slim enough, not fit enough, not strong enough, not rich enough, not beautiful enough, not handsome enough" – the list goes on and on.

It's only natural to want more, that's the way human beings are built. But if we forget about our own successes in life and compare ourselves to celebrities every five minutes, then we're heading down a path of being unhappy for most of our lives.

Try a little experiment with yourself, starting right now for the next 24 hours. When 24 hours is up, ask yourself the question, "Have I spent more time thinking about what I'm grateful for or have I spent more time thinking about what I haven't got? Have I spent more time wishing I could change the past, or do I spend more time thinking about the exciting possibilities for the future?" Sometimes we are so caught up in life that we continue with our daily habits and forget to stop and analyse our thoughts and our actions. Some people will go through their entire life having the same types of thoughts every day, which can lead to a pretty poor life. Our happiness depends on how we look at things, and one of my goals in this book is to help you look at things in a more positive way. Being positive won't deliver all the answers, but it will allow us to live a happier and less stressful life.

We forget the magic and beauty of what's around us.

Take your mind back to your childhood and how much fun you had. As adults, we can take life too seriously, our ego can take over and we then stop living in the moment and enjoying ourselves. We all love achieving things and taking our lives to the next level, but if we're stressed all the time because we're chasing someone else's perception of success, then we are not truly successful. We are sacrificing our happiness just to try and look good on the outside to other people.

Yes, it's cool achieving things in life and getting recognition from people, but we need to look at the bigger picture to see if we are living truly fulfilled lives. Are you playing by your own rules or are you playing by someone else's? Are you chasing your own dream or are you chasing what others perceive as success? Success means different things to different people and we need to achieve our own definition of success to be truly happy and fulfilled in life.

# The Underdog

# CHAPTER 2

# YOUR BODY IS A MIRACLE

*"We celebrate our ability to create machines that
move as a man; yet we take for granted the miracle
that is the human body."*
– David Alejandro Fearnhead

# The Underdog

Whether you love it or hate it, your body is pretty awesome. Here's some info about you that you may or may not know. Hopefully, what you will realise is how incredible and lucky you are to have been given this miracle called life:

Unless you have lost a limb or two, you have 206 bones in your body. Incredibly, ounce for ounce, your bones have a greater pressure tolerance than steel.

Your heart beats around 100,000 times a day, that's over 35 million times a year.

A CNN report stated researchers at Rockefeller University and the Howard Hughes Institute reported that humans can distinguish between 1 trillion smells.

According to the Daily Mail, the human eye can see over 10 million different colours

According to Anne Marie Helmenstine Ph.D, if you put all the DNA molecules in your body end to end, the DNA would reach from the Earth to the Sun and back over 600 times.

Everything is made up of atoms, me, you, water, food, the device you're reading these words on, it's all made up of tiny atoms invisible to the human eye.

If you weigh roughly 70kg (154 lbs) your body is made up of approximately 7 octillion atoms. Which is obviously 7,000,000,000,000,000,000,000,000,000 or 7 billion, billion, billion. OK, maybe not so obvious to either you or me, but this simply states how complex, how genius and how precious you are.

A lot of work has gone into you. Before you even go into self-development and creating a better life for yourself, it's important to look at the work that has already gone into your body. I mention certain engineering structures in this book that have been created by geniuses, but none of these structures are designed anywhere near as impressively as you have been.

What we have already been given as human beings is phenomenal, and to create that great life for ourselves, all we need to do is put a little bit of effort in to get the icing on the cake. OK, let's be realistic here, to excel at something to a very high level we have to put a lot of effort in, but it's still not much effort compared to what you've been given for free.

Although humans have done some pretty stupid things throughout history compared with most of the species on this planet, we are pretty smart. It is estimated by leading scientific authorities that our brains have approximately 100 billion neurones.

We have between 35 – 48 thoughts a minute, which is approximately 50,000 – 70,000 thoughts a day. That's an impressive number. So ask yourself, what are those thoughts? Because your thoughts lead to actions and your actions will create your lifestyle.

It's easy for us to put ourselves down and have negative thoughts, but it's important to take a look at how clever we really are. One of the world's fastest supercomputers that had 82,944 processors took on the power of the human brain. The supercomputer never came close; it took 40 minutes to simulate only 1 second of 1% of our brain activity.

The Underdog

# CHAPTER 3

# STANDING ON THE SHOULDERS OF GIANTS

*"If I have seen further than others, it is by standing upon the shoulders of giants."*
– Sir Isaac Newton

# The Underdog

When it comes down to succeeding at anything in life, we need to look at people who have already been successful at what we want to be successful at. We can avoid making a lot of mistakes by learning from other people who have already worked things out.

On 16 March 1926, American Robert Goddard launched the world's first liquid-fuelled rocket in Auburn, Massachusetts. Although Goddard was a pioneer and achieved something great, Goddard learned from other people to make his dream a reality. One of those people was British scientist Sir Isaac Newton, who came up with his 3rd Law of Motion: "For every action, there is an equal and opposite reaction" which explained the main physics of how a rocket would work.

Even though Newton was a giant in the world of science, he also learned from other people so he could achieve great things. When Newton built the first practical telescope, he would have learned from other people. When Newton and Gottfried Leibniz developed modern calculus, they both learned from other people first.

Although great inventors, physicists and scientists like Sir Isaac Newton, Galileo Galilei, Nikola Tesla, Charles Darwin, Marie Curie, Archimedes, Alexander Fleming, Thomas Edison, Stephen Hawking and Albert Einstein are all considered geniuses, they all started off with 1 + 1 and learned from other people.

Learning from people who have excelled in their field can save you weeks, months, and sometimes even years of wasted effort. If you're anything like me, you will want to achieve your goals sooner rather than later.

When I went on the Commando Course, I had put a lot of training in so I could achieve my dream of getting the Green Beret. Unfortunately, I didn't ask any Commandos for their advice on the best type of training to do, and one of the key things that I never worked on was endurance. I worked on my upper body and I was putting in a lot of runs in for training, but the runs were too short. If I knew back then what I now know, I would have done longer runs to get used to the endurance tests that would come along on the Commando Course.

As a result, my endurance was relatively weak, and I suffered far more than I would have done if I had put the proper training in.

You may not have access to high achievers on the start of your journey, but you can always read books or blogs written by someone who has done what you want to do and how they did it, or you can read biographies to learn about how they think and how they have overcome challenges in their lives.

A word of caution: there are lots of people out there who will want to give you their advice on something. They can talk with tremendous confidence and they can be very convincing, which could lead you to make a bad decision. Just because someone talks with supreme confidence about a subject, it doesn't mean they are right about it. How many people have started a business with tons of confidence and failed? And how many politicians have we seen over the years that have convinced millions of people to follow "their way" and things have ended up going badly wrong?

This is one of the reasons why I started interviewing high achievers. I wanted to learn from these people and I also wanted to share their words of wisdom so other people could learn from them too.

One of my goals is to be a successful author. Looking at my level of education and my track record with writing, most people would write me off (excuse the pun); again, I am an underdog and my chances look slim to most people. In fact, if I told certain members of my family, they would think I'm crazy and dismiss it immediately. They would look at my track record and think "the facts are, Mark hasn't achieved anything in the writing world, so he's got no chance, it's just one of his silly little dreams". But all high achievers know that the facts can be changed if your dream is big enough and you take action and the right steps towards your dream. I don't have time to waste getting involved in family disputes, it's also a negative drain on my energy so I avoid it, and just get on with trying to achieve what I want to achieve.

When it comes to writing, publishing and marketing a book, am I going to take advice from people who aren't doing well with selling books, or am I going to take advice from people who have been through what I'm going through and have come out the other end super successful? The answer is obvious; I'm going to take the advice of the super successful ones. Unfortunately, I didn't always take their advice, and guess what, it didn't turn out well for me.

Sometimes you just have to screw up and learn certain things the hard way.

When it comes to learning about writing, publishing, and marketing books, the three main podcasts I listen to are created by Steve Scott, Mark Dawson, and Joanna Penn. Not only are they all doing incredibly well with their own writing, publishing, and marketing businesses, they also have guests on their podcasts who consistently make six and sometimes seven-figure incomes through selling their books. Yes, yes it's not all about money but given the options of:

1. Making lots of mistakes vs. making few mistakes.

2. Wasting lots of time vs. being productive with my time.

3. Making very little money vs. making lots of money, it's probably best to take the latter options, because...

A. It's less stressful.

B. I get quicker results.

C. I get more freedom to do the things I want to do with my family and friends.

When you listen to experts, sometimes the advice can be confusing because there can be a difference of opinion, so there can be more than one way to be successful. But there are certain things which they all agree on, and it's vital to take that advice.

When it comes to being a successful author, most experts agree that one or even two books aren't enough. You have to keep producing book after book, and the more books you produce, the better the results you will get. Although I've been slow in producing this book, I've already written most of the content for my second book, Delusions of Grandeur. But I know even that's not enough, so I've produced over 70 pages of another self-development book, over 30 pages of my autobiography, there's a whole load of content from my interviews that can be put into several books and I have ideas for even more.

If you want to go deeper into life, there are also people from the world of philosophy and religion who you can learn from.

Some philosophy is good and some not so good. Some religious teachings are good and some not so good. As Shakespeare said, "there is nothing either good or bad, but thinking makes it so."

Ultimately, it's down to us what we decided to believe or not believe. But if you are aiming to improve other people's lives as well as your own, you won't go far wrong.

So when you want to achieve something, whatever it is, always find someone who has the experience with the success and learn from them.

Stand on the shoulders of giants, achieve your dreams, and become a giant yourself!

Learn from giants to propel you to the next level.

# The Underdog

# CHAPTER 4

## THE BRIDGE OF LIFE

*"Sometimes, if you aren't sure about something, you just have to jump off the bridge and grow your wings on the way down."*

– Danielle Steel

# The Underdog

There are several different definitions for a bridge, but the main ones are:

- "A structure that is built over a road, or a chasm to allow people to cross from one side to the other."

- "Something that makes it easier to make a change from one situation to the other."

Any of us that have goals and dreams in life first think up the dream and then think, "How am I going to get from one side to the other?"

What is certain with any big goal is that there will be big challenges that lay ahead when you want to achieve them.

There will be times in your life when you're heading towards your goal and everything is great. The sun will be shining, and you can see your destination.

These are great times but savour them and enjoy them as much as you can, because at some point things will go wrong. This isn't negative thinking; this is just the way life goes: nobody sails through life without any challenges. And just like with the Golden Gate Bridge, the fog will close in and you will no longer be able to see your destination.

These times are the times of uncertainty, and they can also be the most dangerous for you. These situations occur in life not only when you're striving for a goal but also with things that are not directly linked to your goals, for example, a relationship unexpectedly ending or the death of a loved one. These are the times when the fog can come in thick, you think you know where you are, but you can no longer see the beauty that was there before. All of a sudden you're no longer on solid ground, but you're hundreds of feet up in the air, not knowing what might hit you next.

Sometimes you may have to slow down when you are in the fog of life. Sometimes you will be going slower than you originally planned. If that happens, you will get to your destination slower than you expected, but if you keep going, you'll get there.

I missed the original launch date for this book, which was frustrating, and I felt I had not only let people down but had let myself down, too. I had been slow with getting this book published, as lots of other things were demanding my attention. But even at a slow pace, I kept on going. And sometimes that's all you need to do in life to succeed.

Building a great life, in many ways, is the same as building an impressive structure or a great bridge. It takes effort, dedication, and determination to create something strong and impressive. And when you take on a project that has never been done before, there are many people who will doubt your ability to succeed.

Just like when I set out to achieve many of my goals, the team that built the Akashi-Kaikyo Bridge had many doubters. People doubted that they could build a suspension bridge so tough and so long.

The Akashi-Kaikyo Bridge is (at the time of writing) the pinnacle of bridge engineering. It is the longest suspension bridge in the world, with a central span of 1,991 metres and an overall length of 3,911 metres with two main supporting towers.

It can withstand typhoon winds of up to 178 mph, harsh sea currents, tsunamis and earthquakes measuring up to magnitude 8.5. It's a marvel of modern engineering!

The reason it exists today is because it is based on technology from seven other bridges. The engineers stood on the shoulders of giants and learned from the engineers of the past. They adapted past things and made them better than they've ever been.

This can be related to your life. Many people tend to go through life trying to find their own way through things without learning from the people who have gone before them and who have created great lives for themselves and other people.

When I say great things, I mean what you consider great. It might be passing a certain test, running 5k or learning to walk again after an accident. We all have our own levels of what we think a great accomplishment is: if it's something we feel proud of, then that's good; but if it's something we feel proud of and it brings value to someone else's life, that's brilliant!

Robert F. Kennedy said it best when he said:

*"Few people will have the greatness to bend history itself, but each of us can work to change a small portion of events. It is from numberless diverse acts of courage and belief that human history is shaped. Each time a man stands up for an ideal, or acts to improve the lot of others, or strikes out against injustice, he sends forth a tiny ripple of hope and crossing each other from*

*a million different centres of energy. Those ripples build a current which can sweep down the mightiest of oppression and resistance."*

# CHAPTER 5

# BUILDING MENTAL STRENGTH

*"Our greatest glory is not in never falling, but in rising
every time we fall."*
– Confucius

# The Underdog

If you have ever been over a suspension bridge like the Severn Bridge connecting Wales to England or the Golden Gate Bridge in California, you will notice there are huge steel cables supporting the bridge.

The cables look like one long thick cable going from end to end, but in fact they're made up of many different cables. On the Akashi-Kaikyo Bridge there are 36,830 strands of steel wire, each wire 112cm (44 inches). The big cables you can see weigh about 25,000 tones and contain enough wire to circle the Earth seven times... the overall length of the wire is 190,000 miles!

These steel wires combined hold up the bridge, and as I mentioned earlier, it can withstand huge earthquakes, tsunamis, and typhoons. It is without question one of the most advanced bridges in the world.

It is the same with building a great life and having happiness and confidence. These things are not formed in one event; they are formed in thousands of hours and experiences. Each positive experience we have is like a steel wire. When we are committed to being optimistic about things and we have another positive experience, it is like two steel wires combining and becoming stronger. It is the same with habits, the more success we have with new positive habits the more overall success we will have. Success breeds success!

In 1995, before the bridge was fully completed, the Great Hanshin earthquake (also known as the Kobe earthquake) hit and destroyed much of the area surrounding the Akashi-Kaikyo. The earthquake was devastating! It measured a whopping 7 on the Seismic Intensity Scale. Over 5,000 people were killed, over 36,000 people were injured, over 250,000 people were displaced, and it caused approximately $200 billion worth of damage.

So what happened to the Akashi-Kaikyo Bridge that was in the thick of it all? When structures all over the city were collapsing as easily as we can kick a sandcastle over, the Akashi-Kaikyo stood firm and survived. It was scarred from the devastating event, but it never collapsed, and to this day it still stands tall. When it comes to being tough, there are very few structures that are as tough as the Akashi-Kaikyo. The bridge was well thought out; thousands upon thousands of hours went into it being made, so planning is vital to success.

*"It does not do to leave a live dragon out of your calculations, if you live near him."*
– J. R. R. Tolkien (Author of 'Lord of the Rings')

It was made of special materials, and for that reason it didn't collapse when something devastating happened in the area.

It is like that in life: at some point in our life our mental world will be shaken up. Something will happen that can shake us at our very foundation, but if we are trained enough mentally and if we are strong enough, we will get through it.

So the more we feed our minds with positive material and thoughts, the stronger we will become and the better we will handle our own personal earthquakes, tsunamis, and typhoons in life.

The late, great motivational speaker and author Jim Rohn talked about the seasons of life. You will have springs, summers, autumns, and winters in life, that is inevitable. Jim Rohn is right; the hard times will come so prepare well but remember this:

*"Iron doesn't become steel until it goes through the fire."*

You can choose to get stronger or you can choose to break.

Many people think that this choice is out of our hands, but we and we alone are responsible for how we decide to handle a situation.

Taking responsibility for our actions is thought of by many top achievers to be a sign of human maturity. It is what separates the men from the boys and the women from the girls. You and you alone are responsible for your mental attitude, even though you may not be responsible for what has happened to you. There are circumstances in life that happen to us which we simply have no control over, but we can control how we act when life kicks us in the balls.

Maybe there have been times in your life when you've felt secure in your job and then one day you get told you are no longer needed: "Bye bye!" You think, "Oh, great, now how am I going to pay for food, my rent, my mortgage, my car, the gas, the electric, the loans I have, etc?"

It is natural to think about all of those things and you may feel worried. But we have to remember that it is us that controls our thoughts regardless of the event. You can decide to interpret things so they will be to your advantage.

In 2013, I was mistakenly sectioned and locked up in a mental health ward. To cut a long story short, I was assessed on my mental health by four assessors and without them talking to any of my friends and family about me, they locked me up. I was unjustly shipped 52 miles away from my home and found myself staring at a wall in a mental health facility. Ironically, I felt incredibly strong mentally and had great mental health, so it was one of the most bizarre experiences of my life.

As I stood staring at the wall, I looked at this as a test. Rather than thinking, "Why me?" I thought, "Game on mother fuckers!"

I ended up breaking out of the facility, found myself on the run from the police, but in the end I claimed my freedom. I was later given a letter saying words to the effect of, "Mark shows no sign of mental health issues."

When I read the letter I thought, "No shit Sherlock, my friends and family could have told you guys that before you locked me up."

The point here is I decided to take control of the situation in my mind. I couldn't control what had happened, but I could control the thoughts I was having, and by controlling my own thoughts I came through winning in the end. You can do the same when life throws you a curve ball.

They say that out of every negative situation can come

some benefit, and this was true in this case. I got to test how strong I was mentally, and I thought more clearly than probably any other time in my life. I had to get out of the situation. It also led to me completing another endurance challenge straight after I got out. And best of all, I've written a book about the experience.

# CHAPTER 6

# IT DOESN'T MATTER WHERE YOU START FROM – IT MATTERS WHERE YOU'RE GOING

*"I would visualise things coming to me. It would just make me feel better. Visualisation works if you work hard. That's the thing. You can't just visualise and go eat a sandwich."*
– Jim Carrey

# The Underdog

I didn't do well in school, but school is really only the starting point of learning. Many people think like I did: if you don't do well in school then you're not going to do well in life.

This couldn't be further from the truth. If you've done well in school; then that can be a bonus that may lead you on to other things.

You could have two people, one brilliant academically but lacking drive and creativity, the other not as good academically but with lots of drive and creativity. The academic person could go on to achieve very little and the creative go-getter could go onto achieve great things. A perfect example of this is Richard Branson.

Generally, the person that succeeds is the guy or the girl who sets goals, is willing to learn, is focused and has lots of determination.

When I wanted to improve myself I read books, listened to cassette tapes, CDs and now YouTube and podcasts about how to achieve things. It is hardly rocket science; it may sound obvious to do this, but many people simply will not do it. They go to their 9-5 jobs and learn what they have to for their jobs, but when work is over they sit down in front of the TV and flick through the channels to see if they can find some form of entertainment to stop them from becoming bored.

There's nothing wrong with this, and it is not for me to judge what another person does with their life, but if you want to achieve on a high level, then you will need to invest your time in educating your mind rather than watching hours upon hours of TV every night.

One of the main reasons I've done so well in running is because I put the time into my training. I started out with very little fitness and after seeing me fail my 1.5 mile Army basic fitness test, you would have written me off as a decent runner. But I wasn't focused on my lack of fitness; I was focused on getting better. I wasn't focused on where I was; I was focused on where I was going. I had no idea that I would achieve so much, but I just kept on achieving one goal at a time. Every time I got to one level, I could see a bit further and think about going to the next level. The Chinese saying, "A journey of a thousand miles begins with a single step" is true.

In 2001, I decided to go for the 100k Treadmill World Record. There are many different ways to achieve a goal, and the way I decided to tackle this goal was to run 10k at a time.

When running a long distance like this you have to take in lots of water and, ideally, electrolytes. Electrolytes are mainly made up of sodium, potassium, magnesium, and calcium. They maintain the body's fluid balance and carry electrical energy to help the body function properly. Without these vital ingredients you can get cramps, weaker muscles, fatigue, dizziness, muscle spasms and a few other unpleasant things. Granted, if you're pushing your body you could get these things anyway, but taking on enough electrolytes will lessen the risk and keep your body working more efficiently. This all goes back to planning being vital to success.

Because I was talking in so much water and electrolyte drink, I would need to go for a pee every hour. This came in very handy for my 10k at a time goal. I would run 10k and then go to the loo (another top tip: make sure your pee is a fairly clear colour. If it's dark yellow, it means you're dehydrated, and you will lose a lot of performance). So I was focused only doing 10k runs at an easy pace, which was a strategy that worked well.

At the end of the run, I had comfortably broken the World

Record. My legs were a bit tight, but I felt pretty good overall, and knew I could have run another marathon on top of the 100k. I had prepared well, and I was focused on where I was going.

With the Sahara Desert 130-miler over 6 days, I used a different strategy. We all set off in the morning and the only thought in my mind was, "I'm going to keep running all day until I get there." That strategy also worked.

With the 1600-mile run in the United States, I usually just ran until I hit a town or a certain campsite.

And with the Strava Distance Challenge, I just worked my way up until I came 1st on the leader board.

So there was no single strategy that worked: lots of strategies worked, but they all had one thing in common. I was focused on where I was going and not where I was.

It can be the same thing with what you take on in life. There may be more than one way to achieve your goal, but the main thing to do is... focus on where you're going, not where you are.

# CHAPTER 7

# CRITICS

*"There is only one way to avoid criticism:*
*Do nothing, Say nothing, Be nothing."*
– Aristotle

# The Underdog

If your goal is to make a better life for yourself and your family, I can guarantee you one thing: you will attract critics. The minute you announce that you are going to go for a big goal is the minute when you leave yourself open to criticism. It's just part of life.

The one thing you can take comfort from is that every single person who has achieved great things in their life has had critics. When Sam Walton started Walmart, you can bet your bottom dollar that people thought he was going to fail. Walmart later became the most successful supermarket chain in the world, with profits exceeding $14 billion a year and the largest business employer in the world, with more than 2.3 million employees. Even though Sam had the right to say, "I told you so", it wouldn't really matter, because whether you are rich or poor, fat or thin, good or bad, some people will still criticise you, it never ends.

I've even attracted the odd critic with my interviews. I

remember someone on YouTube called me a Welsh twat, another person said I was no Jonathan Ross, and another person called me an absolute c**t!

If you want to achieve more out of life, then you will get more criticism. It's just the way things are, when you stick your head out of the crowd; expect to get a few tomatoes thrown at it.

Some of the most popular shows on TV today are things like American Idol, X-Factor and Britain/America's Got Talent. They do provide great entertainment; some people turn out to be amazing, and some are not so amazing. It's pretty easy to sit in the audience and laugh at some of the acts that come on, and I have to admit myself, that sometimes I think, "maybe it's time you tried something else, mate." So some criticism can be good.

There are basically two types of critic, those who have a genuine interest in helping you succeed in life and use constructive criticism and those who, no matter what you do, want to tear you down and see you fail. The challenging bit can be telling the difference between the two, because if you do not get this right it could mean the difference between success and failure.

Generally, people believe that friends that they have known for a long time will have their best interests at heart and will give them valuable support and advice. But before you take advice from any friends or family, you have to decide if they want to see you achieve your dreams. You must also look at the fruit on their tree to see if they have achieved what you want to achieve before you take advice from them. There are also those people who care about you who will try to suppress your dreams simply because they do not want you to be disappointed if you fail. I love my mum dearly and I know she loves me, but that does not mean I should take advice from her when it comes to living my life. If my mum had her way, I would have a 9-5 job for the next 30 years doing any job to get by, even if it was something that I didn't enjoy.

But settling for a job that I don't like has never been part of my game plan in life, and if you're in a job you don't like, get a new one. You may read that sentence and think "that's easier said than done, because I have bills to pay". There's a lot of truth in that, and I know I've taken jobs I didn't really love just to pay the bills and get by. If it's a temporary thing, that's fine, but if you're not happy in your job, you need to start looking for other possibilities. The danger for many people is they take a job temporarily and then they get stuck in that job for the next 5, 10 or even 20 years. Before they realised what's happened, they've wasted a massive chunk of their lives.

If you want to take the safe options in life, that's fine. You won't attract as many critics, but the downside to that is you will never achieve your potential and you could end up asking yourself the worst question in the word... "What if ?"

There are those people that will hate to see you succeed and be happy. For one reason or another they want to see you crash and burn. In fact, if something goes badly wrong in your life, there are people who would feel good about you failing. It is like the bully Nelson from The Simpsons TV show who points and says "HAHA" when something goes wrong.

We all have our Nelsons in our lives, but the key here is to not let them win. Yes, you will trip up and fail at certain things, and yes you will have people who doubt you, but if you listen to the critics, you may live to regret not being bold and just going for your dream.

Some people will tell you why you won't succeed, and other people will tell other people about how foolish you are to have your dream.

I recently came across this. The author is unknown, and it is apparently an experience that the Greek philosopher Socrates went through. Where it's from and how true it is I don't know, but I think there is something to be learned in this message.

In ancient Greece, Socrates was visited by an acquaintance. Eager to share some juicy gossip, the man asked if Socrates would like to hear the story he'd just heard about a friend of theirs. Socrates replied that before the man spoke, he needed to pass the "Triple-Filter" test.

The first filter, he explained, is Truth. "Have you made absolutely sure that what you are about to say is true?"

The man shook his head. "No, I actually just heard about it, and..." Socrates cut him off. "You don't know for certain that it is true, then. Is what you want to say something good or kind?"

Again, the man shook his head. "No! Actually, just the opposite. You see..."

Socrates lifted his hand to stop the man speaking. "So, you are not certain that what you want to say is true, and it isn't good or kind. One filter still remains, though, so you may yet still tell me. That is Usefulness or Necessity. Is this information useful or necessary to me?"

A little defeated, the man replied, "No, not really."

"Well, then," Socrates said, turning on his heel, "If what you want to say is neither true, nor good or kind, nor useful or necessary, please don't say anything at all."

You have probably come across this type of critic in your own life.

Life is too short to go around saying bad things about people and criticising other people all the time. If you focus on something negative, then the chances are you will become negative about life and people. Look for the good in people and avoid people who have only got bad things to say about everyone.

# CHAPTER 8

# YOU ARE LUCKY

*"Be thankful for what you have; you'll end up having more.
If you concentrate on what you don't have, you will never,
ever have enough."*
– Oprah Winfrey

# The Underdog

Many people think to themselves, "I wish I was lucky; I wish something great would happen in my life," but the reality is there are always great things happening in your life. There are always miracles, but sometimes we take things for granted so we forget to see the little miracles. When I see my son Léon, I am in awe of the little miracle that is running around by my feet laughing and playing. When Léon calls me Daddy, it's just the best. When everything goes pear-shaped, I can take a step back and think about Léon and how lucky I am to have him in my life. But it is not just Léon that I am amazed by; there are many things to be grateful for. Good health has got to be the most important thing to be grateful for. Without health, life can be pretty miserable. You are living in a machine that is priceless. $100 billion could not create another person as unique as you, and sometimes we need to remember that.

When it comes to life expectancy, if you live in the Central African Republic, Sierra Leone, Zimbabwe or Zambia, your life expectancy is 45 to 46 years on average.

Compare this to countries like the UK, New Zealand, Australia, the US, Canada, France, and Japan which have an average life expectancy of 79 to 84 years. If you're from the western world, the chances are you're going to live a lot longer than if you live in certain other countries, so count your lucky stars.

When we look at the technology and the luxuries we have today, it is astounding to compare what we have now to what people had years ago. I was recently watching one of my favourite Leonardo DiCaprio movies, "The Great Gatsby". There are people in the movie who are extremely wealthy, but what they had back then pales in comparison to what we have now. They may have had a bigger house, more land and a few more diamonds than most people would have today, but today we have so many items that people of 100 years ago could only dream about.

If you live in the developed world, then chances are you have access to most of the things available today. A hundred years ago there were no Samsung smartphones, no iPads, no computers, no microwaves, no DVD players, no Internet, no cheap flights abroad, no YouTube, no Google, no Facebook, no Twitter, no Skype, no digital cameras, no Amazon shopping, and no TVs.

We live better today than any king could have years ago: you don't need to go that far back to when they did not even have sewage systems in place. No toilets, no electricity, no gas, no cars, no roads, no planes, no helicopters, and no supermarkets with all of your food in one place.

Although all of these modern-day conveniences are great, the quality of your life is not governed by the things you have. The quality of your life is based on your emotional stability and the thoughts you think about yourself and what you think about your life.

If a billionaire thinks they are lacking something and focusing on what they have not got, then they may not be as happy as people think they would be. The trappings of success may look good from the outside, and it is certainly better to have some money than none, but if they are not happy, the person who has very little materially but who feels they have an abundance of good things has a far better mental state.

What we say to ourselves determines our actions, and our actions determine the outcome of our lives. Many people have no idea what they are doing when they are talking to themselves. It is so easy to put yourself down and talk negatively about yourself, but if you do this consistently, you will create a negative thought process that will lead to negative actions.

By believing that you are lucky, and you are a winner, you create a self-fulfilling prophecy. If you have low self-esteem like I once had, it may seem like you are lying to yourself, but the more you repeat this; the more you will start winning, and the more you start to win, the more of a winner you will become. You'll then get to a point where you just believe that you are a winner and things are going to work out for you. Life is not designed to let you win all the time, there will be good times and there will be hard times, but you can choose how you want to feel in the hard times.

Sometimes I hear people say negative words to themselves with a "Why me, poor old me?" attitude.

They feel sorry for themselves and have found comfort in playing the victim role. They moan and groan about anything and everything. They struggle to understand why life isn't going well for them and think the winners in life are just lucky. Yes, there is luck in life, but we make most of our luck ourselves. So rather than blame people all the time, we must take responsibility and take back control of our lives.

Yes, it's easier said than done, but it can be done. There are millions of people out there in the world who are living great lives. They have discovered the so-called Secret to Success, the secret to living a great live and being happy. If you want to be happy then look at all the things you have to be grateful for, enjoy the journey (not just the destination) and decide to be happy right now. Not tomorrow, not when you achieve your next goal, decide to be happy now.

In the chapter "Your Body Is A Miracle" you've read about how amazing you are and how powerful the human brain is. Remember that you are the person who is in charge of your brain, so point it in the direction you want to go and be happy now.

I recently watched the movie The Pianist for the first time and decided to watch Schindler's List again. Both films are an insight to what happened to certain groups of people during The Holocaust. Approximately 6 million people were mass- murdered, they were mainly Jewish but other persecuted groups including gays and Gypsies were beaten and ruthlessly executed.

While writing this book, I thought back to when I visited Auschwitz and Oscar Schindler's factory in Poland. I also thought about the time when I visited Anne Frank's house in Amsterdam in the Netherlands.

I thought about how lucky we are not to have gone through that. Sometimes we will hear on the news that there has been another mass shooting in America, or another terrorist attack somewhere. This can put some people into a state of fear, but it's nothing compared to the fear that we would have faced in a Nazi death camp. I have no doubt that there were many brave and tough people in the camps, but imagine how you would feel if you saw your loved one separated from you and you never saw them again.

You will see many people in the world of self-development claim to have made themselves successful solely through their own thoughts. While there is some truth in that, there is also luck involved. We have no control with what part of the world we were born in and no control what era it was in.

So always be grateful for what you have been given already. And even if you are facing challenging times right now, remember you are stronger than any challenge that will come your way!

# CHAPTER 9

# PERSPECTIVE

*"There are no facts, only interpretations."*
– Friedrich Nietzsche

# The Underdog

Think you have always had it tough because of lack of money? Yes, it can be very difficult to get by without enough money, and to make many of our dreams come true we need money. But when we are feeling sorry for ourselves because we have not got enough, it may be worth putting things in perspective before we mentally beat ourselves up.

Let us take a look at things from a different perspective and see how many of us in the western world measure up to other countries in terms of having money.

According to dosomething.org:

- Nearly half of the world's population, that is more than 3 billion people live on less than $2.50 a day, and more than 1.3 billion people live in extreme poverty, that is, they live on less than $1.25 a day.

- 1 billion children worldwide are living in poverty

and according to UNICEF 22,000 children die each day due to poverty

- 805 million people worldwide do not have enough food to eat.

- 663 million people lack access to safe water and 1/3 of the global population live without access to a toilet, according to Matt Damon's charity water.org

So when we look at things on a world scale, many of us are a lot better off than we think.

BEING IN THE TOP 1% OF EARNERS IN THE WORLD

Being a top earner on a global scale may not be as hard as you think if you live in a developed country.

At the time of writing there is a great website called www.globalrichlist.net where you can type in your annual net income and find out where you stand compared to the rest of the world.

If you earn:

- £10,000 a year, you are in the top 12.2%. Out of over 7 billion people on the planet that puts you comfortably in the top 730 million highest income earners on Earth.

- £15,000 a year, you are in the top 4.1%. Out of over 7 billion people on the planet that puts you comfortably in the top 250 million highest income earners on Earth.

- £20,000 a year, you are in the top 2%. Out of over 7 billion people on the planet that puts you comfortably in the top 115 million highest income earners on Earth.

- £25,500 a year, you are in the top 1%. Out of over 7 billion people on the planet that puts you comfortably in the top 60 million highest income earners on Earth.

If you are like me and you live in a super-rich country, you will tend to see the odd glossy magazine with celebrities in. So just in case you are thinking what percentage they are in, let's take a look at a few other figures. If they (or you) earn:

- £100,000 a year, they will be in the top 0.07%. Out of over 7 billion people they will be in the top 4.1 million highest income earners in the world.

- £1 million net income a year, they will be in the top

0.008% and out of 7 billion people they will be in the top half a million highest income earners in the world.

- If you are David Beckham and earned £50.8 million in 2015 (according to express.co.uk) and are one of the highest earning retired athletes (according to Forbes.com), you are in the top 0.0001%. It's a tough life for some, but he does have a beautiful smile.

OK, that is money at an extreme level, but just because you are not earning David's type of money; it does not mean that you're not doing well financially.

If you are not working at the moment and you are over 25 and living in the UK and are claiming benefits (obviously it will vary for different countries and there are different types of benefits), you would be on roughly £73 a week which is £3,796 a year. You would be in the top 24% highest earners in the world without even working.

Yes, things are relative to what country you live in and food is probably cheaper in poorer countries, but if many of the people in the poorest countries (like the Central African Republic, the Democratic Republic of the Congo or Malawi) want to buy a Samsung Galaxy smartphone, an iPad, or a car, things can be a little more challenging, unless of course they become one of the higher income earners in their country.

I remember the time I lost my job; I woke up the next day and thought, "I cannot believe I am in this situation at this point in my life". Whatever happened to the large amounts of money I thought I would earn and had not made happen? I checked my bank balance, and I had £3.15. Even my son had more money than me, as a few years earlier I had put over £4,000 in his trust fund when I was earning a lot more than I did when I wrote the very first edition on this book. It was quite comical, really, but many people get so depressed about their financial situation it can lead them to a very dark place and some sadly even turn to suicide.

Even when it looks like you have lost a lot, there is still so much to be grateful for. On this particular day, I was up in the morning and putting my cereal in the bowl ready to have my breakfast. I thought to myself, "Hey, you still have a roof over your head, you are not going to go hungry, you still live in one of the greatest countries in the world and you are healthy enough to find work, even if it's to just get by for now". There is no need to compare yourself to the Beckham's of this world.

If you live in a developed country, you will still probably be in the top 25% income earners in the world, and if you are not in a developed country, then there are still lots of possibilities where you can change your circumstances and make a better life for yourself.

Everyone without exception who has made a dream a reality has suffered some sort of failure before they made that dream that reality. Here are a few examples of people who have failed and then turned things around to become successful.

One schoolboy was cut from his high school basketball team. His dream was to be a pro basketball player, so this was devastating to him. A setback like this would have put doubt in even the most confident person. He was so upset with being cut from the team, he went back to his house, locked himself in his room and cried. But he decided to pick himself back up and work harder than he had ever worked before. He not only went on to become a pro basketball player, he became a six-times NBA Champion, and became arguably the greatest basketball player of all time. That little boy's name was Michael Jordan.

*"I've missed more than 9000 shots in my career. I've lost almost 300 games. 26 times I've been trusted to take the game-winning shot and missed. I've failed over and over and over again in my life. And that is why I succeed."*
– Michael Jordan

One little boy was a late starter in life, and he couldn't speak until the age of 4.

In school he did badly, and he failed his university exams.

But being a slow starter and failing exams did not stop this boy.

Later his work helped develop atomic energy, and he became the most influential physicist of the 20th century.

His name was Albert Einstein.

# CHAPTER 10

# STORIES – FROM FAILURE TO SUCCESS

*"Try not to become a man of success, but rather try to become a man of value."*
– Albert Einstein

# The Underdog

One boy did not do well in school; his parents thought little of him, he spoke with a lisp and stuttered.

His name was Winston Churchill.

> *"If you're going through hell, keep going."*
> – Winston Churchill

One man was sacked from working for a local newspaper and was told he had no original ideas. He wanted to set up a park where children could go with their parents so the whole family could have fun. He also set up an animation studio that went bankrupt. Banks turned him away because they did not believe in him or his dream. Today, one of his parks employees around 62,000 people, and is 40 square miles in size; that's roughly the size of San Francisco. That man's name was Walt Disney.

*"It's kind of fun to do the impossible."*
– Walt Disney

One woman wrote a book and was rejected by 12 publishers. People did not believe in her or her book, but she kept on trying. She kept on asking people to publish her book. When a publisher eventually said they would publish her book, they also advised her to get a job because they believed she would not make much money. Her name is Jo Rowling AKA J. K. Rowling – author of Harry Potter.

*"You might never fail on the scale I did. But it is impossible to live without failing at something, unless you live so cautiously that you might as well not have lived at all in which case, you failed by default."*
– J. K. Rowling

One boy was cut from his team because the coaches thought he was too small, and he lacked the necessary skills to be a good football player. He later became the only player in history to win five FIFA Ballon d'Or's which was an award for the best football player in the world. His name is Lionel Messi.

*"You have to fight to reach your dream. You have to sacrifice and work hard for it."*
– Lionel Messi

One guy had a dream of making great movies, so he decided to apply to get into the University of California film school but was rejected twice. His name was Steven Spielberg.

*"You shouldn't dream your film; you should make it."*
– Steven Spielberg

One man failed in business, his fiancée died, and he lost 8 elections. His name was Abraham Lincoln.

*"The best way to predict the future is to create it."*
– Abraham Lincoln

One band was rejected by a recording studio who said they did not like their music, and they had no future in the music industry. The band ignored the criticism and carried on. Later they sold more singles and had more

Number 1 albums than any other British act. According to the Recording Industry Association of America, they are the best-selling music artists in the US, and they hit the top spot with Billboard Magazine as the most successful of all time. They received 10 Grammy Awards, 15 Ivor Novello Awards, and an Academy Award. They are the most successful band of all time and have sold over 600 million records worldwide. Their names were Paul McCartney, Ringo Starr, George Harrison, and John Lennon... AKA The Beatles.

*"I don't work at being ordinary."*
– Paul McCartney

*"Love one another."*
– Ringo Starr

*"I want to deal with what's in front of me now to the best of my abilities. In the end it is better to go for something and fail than to not go for it and live with regret."*
– George Harrison

*"Imagine."*
– John Lennon

# CHAPTER 11

# GOING COMMANDO – THE WINNING MIND-SET

*"Never give in. Never give in. Never, never, never, never."*
– Winston Churchill

When you read self-development books, you will normally find that high achievers have a certain way of thinking. There are certain things they do; they have certain habits, and they think a certain way when it comes to how they'll achieve their goal.

It's never been so easy to access all of the latest information that will help you achieve your goals. When it comes to being a success at anything, it all boils down to hunger, how badly you want it and whether you're willing to go the extra mile to get what you want.

When I wanted to become a Commando and earn my Green Beret, the odds were massively against me. I wasn't the fittest, I wasn't the most intelligent intellectually, I wasn't the best at solving certain challenges and I wasn't the most confident.

What I was, though, was very, very hungry! I wanted that Green Beret as much if not more than any other person on my course, and as far as I was concerned, nothing and no one was going to stop me. When other people from my Junior Leader regiment had finished their work for the day, I was out training. When it was hot, I was out training. When it was cold, I was out training. When it was windy, I was out training... And when it was hailing, ah, I'm being completely honest with this book. When it was hailing... I took it as a sign to take a rest day and have a nice cup of hot chocolate.

But all jokes aside, you know when someone is really hungry for something because their effort shows up in their daily activity.

One of the big reasons many people fail to achieve their dreams is because they are afraid to take action because they fear failure. Ironically, by not taking action, they fail automatically. Many people do not even try to chase their dreams because they fear failing and looking like a fool.

Having failed the basic Army fitness test only 11 months before and having been voted fattest person in the troop, I looked a very unlikely, if not impossible candidate to pass this elite military course. Out of roughly 120 people in Junior Leaders Regiment, approximately 10 would attempt the course and only two, maybe three, would pass. The odds that I would pass the Commando Course and get into 29 Commando were slim, to say the least.

One of the reasons I wanted to be a Commando was because my cousin Martin Beckerleg was a Commando (serving with 40 Commando and Commando Logistic Regiment) and when I joined Junior Leaders Regiment Royal Artillery, I noticed there were certain staff in the regiment that were (at least that's what I thought) a cut above the rest. Although there were many good Sergeants in Junior Leaders, the ones that stood out the most were the ones that wore the Commando Green Beret and the maroon Para beret. I thought of these guys as special because they had passed tough courses that not anybody could do. They had passed courses that many people have failed, and that was the reason many people wanted to be in one of those regiments. Not everybody would try to get in these regiments, but given the choice, most of the junior soldiers I knew would love to be Commando or Para trained. One of the main reasons was because these guys were respected.

The main man on camp was a Scottish sergeant by the name of Eddie Reid. There were other people in the regiment that had a higher rank, more qualification badges, and more medals than Eddie, but the special thing about Eddie was he was the person in that regiment who had a Commando Green Beret along with a Commando Dagger badge on his upper left arm. To me this badge was worth 20 other qualification badges if not more, and no rank meant as much as having a Green Beret.

The other thing that I admired about Eddie was he was the fittest Sergeant. I would see Eddie out running and he was going at a much faster pace than I could run. He became a shining light for me as a boy soldier because he was different. In a sea of dark blue Army berets, Eddie's Army beret was green, which made him unique. I never thought about it at the time, but thinking back, Eddie must have also been an underdog when he went on the Commando Course. The reason for this is that Eddie's a fairly short guy, and lots of short people (even if they are super-fit) fail the course because many of them cannot carry the heavy backpacks.

Being strong in the Army can be a good thing, but nobody cares that much about it. In the Army, fitness is king, and the king of all fitness exercises is running. If you're a brilliant runner, you get the most respect. So even though I was rubbish at running, I always admired the fittest guys and dreamed about being one of these super-fit people one day.

I admired the fact that the Commandos were good all-round soldiers. They were good at both upper body and lower body fitness and they could operate in both extremes of hot and cold environments around the world.

When I used to go to the cookhouse (I would later call it 'the galley'), there was a photo on the wall of 29 Commando breaking the Military Marathon World Record.

For me that was it, I had to be a Commando, and I had to get into 29 Commando.

After having failing my basic 1.5-mile run, I'd passed 10 weeks later and got into the Army. By the end of the year I was the fastest in my troop on the 1.5-mile run and I was 6th in the battery out of around 120 people.

I went to the 29 Commando thinking I was pretty fit, but as I got to the top of one level, just like a football league, I was now at the bottom.

I failed the 29 Commando Beat Up twice. I passed the 3rd Beat Up by the skin of my teeth and passed the All Arms Commando Course on the 1st attempt, again, by the skin of my teeth.

The reason I got through it wasn't because I was brilliant, it was because I never gave in. If you want something badly enough, you've got to give it everything you've got and never, never, never, never give in.

# The Underdog

# CHAPTER 12

# WHATEVER IT TAKES

*"Nothing in this world can take the place of persistence. Talent will not; nothing is more common than unsuccessful men with talent. Genius will not; unrewarded genius is almost a proverb. Education will not; the world is full of educated derelicts. Persistence and determination alone are omnipotent."*
– Calvin Coolidge

# The Underdog

In 2014, people kept on telling me how good the Strava GPS app was and that I should download it to keep track of my running. After finishing a run one evening, I decided to finally download the app to see what all the fuss was about. I immediately noticed that it had different challenges you could do. The first one I saw was to see how fast you could run 10k, I had no interest in that. The second was to see how fast you could run a half marathon: again, no interest. Although I have respect for anyone who runs these distances, they weren't distances that appealed to me. I was starting to think that there would be no challenges on there that would be of any interest to me, but finally there it was... "how far could you run in a month". That was it; it was kind of like a Goldilocks and the Three Bears moment. The porridge is too cold; the porridge is too hot... ah, now this porridge is just right.

I was far from being in my best shape, but I had been doing some training. I was only around 75% fit at the time, but I thought I would go for it and see where I would come. There are many people out there who relentlessly train every day, and they always maintain a level of fitness that would be at least 90% of their top level. But that's not me, I train every week but if I'm not training towards something specific, I don't train at a very high level. As long as I'm lean and fairly fit, I'm happy with that.

I knew my fitness wasn't as good as it could be, but I set a goal to get into the top 5%. There were over 40,000 runners, so that meant getting into the top 2,000. I realistically thought the big dream for me would be to get in the top 1%, which would mean getting into the top 400.

The next day I set out on my run. Because I had work and other things to do in the day, I had to fit the running around everything else. After I had finished everything I had to do in the day, I set out on my run, I had no idea how many miles the other runners would do as this challenge was new to me. What I did know was that there would be a lot of people who wanted to do the best they could and rank as high as possible on the leader board, so there would be thousands of people who would want to beat me.

When it comes to running big distances, I have learned that it is better to start off slowly. When I did the

Marathon Des Sables Sahara Desert run, I made the mistake of setting off too fast and started to pay for this lack of experience later in the run. From that day on, I have always preferred to start slowly with big distance runs.

You hear of people hitting the wall in the marathon at around the 18 mile point, but the wall doesn't exist if you have put in enough miles in training, you run the first 18 miles at a sensible pace and you've made sure that you've taken in enough carbohydrates and fluids on board.

Many people doing the marathon will follow a basic training plan which involves doing 3, 7 and 9 milers with the odd half marathon thrown in and a single 20-mile run thrown in before the marathon. This sort of programme is OK if you want to just get through the marathon, but for most of us, generally the more miles we put in the better the result we'll get. The elite marathon runners who get the best times are running anything from 100 to 140 miles a week. That many miles a week is something most of us can actually achieve when we put our minds to it. It may bring you personal best times and will get you to a level where you can beat the vast majority of the people who have entered the marathon, but beating the elite runners is a different story. For that you need the combination of the right training, nutrition, and genetics. If you are like me and weigh around 13.5 stone (189 lbs) it isn't likely you'll be beating a 9 stone elite marathon runner anytime soon. You may not have the greyhound-like speed, but there is a good chance you can do the distance.

When I set off on the first day of the Strava Distance Challenge it was December 1st, 2014. Although the weather can be good sometimes in West Wales, we generally don't have the best weather in December. For much of the run, it was more of a drizzle than rain, but I still got soaked. The weather I love to run in the most is in the heat, the hotter the better! When you are going for your dream, you don't always get perfect conditions, but often you have to make a start and keep going.

I don't remember exactly how many hours I was running for, but I do remember just plodding away and not worrying about the time or distance much. On the first day, I was just out there to get some decent miles in and see if I could get in the top 2,000. After I had been running for several hours, I decided to see where I was on the leader board. At the time of checking I hoped that I would be in the top 20,000 runners, but to my amazement, I was already in the top 400. I couldn't believe that I was already in the top 1%, and this motivated me to keep on going.

Sometimes you will have total belief that you will hit a certain goal and you will miss your goal. Other times you won't be so sure of hitting a goal, and something really cool and unexpected happens out of the blue.

Hitting the top 1% it was a lot easier than I expected, so my next goal was to get into the top 300, and if I was fantastically lucky, I may even finish in the top 150. I ran for another few hours and was thinking to myself, "I wonder if I'm in the top 250." When I synchronised to Strava I was shocked to see that I was now in the top 40. I was so pleased I took a screenshot, as I thought that might never climb that high on the leader board again. Here is another lesson for life.

When you put in slightly more effort than most people you put yourself into a much higher league.

Notice there I use the word "slightly." I had probably spent just a few hours more that day on my goal than many people, but it made a huge difference to the outcome in terms of what percentage group I had put myself into, and it can be the same with you with what you want to excel at.

However, putting yourself into the top 10% may take just a little more effort, but putting yourself into the very high levels means you usually have to put in a lot more effort. The closer you get to the top of the ladder in your chosen field, the more you will come across other people who are also very driven and who will also go the extra mile to be one of the best.

I kept on running again and I stopped to synchronise to Strava. It just kept getting better; I was now at 12th, out of over 40,000 runners. I could have been sensible here, finished at 12th and got some good rest in for the run the next day, but to hell with 12th, I now had to get into the top 10! I thought there will be other people out running so there was a possibility I could move down in the ranking, but the next time I synchronised it, it wasn't the case, as I was now number 6!

Again, I had surpassed my goal and now wanted to get into the top 5. Top 5 sounded good and I had to get into this prestigious group.

I ran until 2.30am, uploaded my miles and found out that I was now in 3rd place. I had gone through over 40,000 runners to 3rd, and this should have been enough for me. But I had come too far to come 3rd. It was cold and wet, and I was soaked to the skin, but I had to keep going.

While I was doing this run, my Uncle/Dad (who brought me up from a baby) Des was in hospital and in a bad way with a tracheotomy. He had smoked, drank (though not to excess, just a few a night) and eaten unhealthy for years and it had finally caught up with him. We didn't know if he would make it out alive.

During my time on the December Strava Challenge, I sometimes went up to the hospital to see him outside visiting hours. Although I wasn't extremely close to Des, I did love him and I always appreciated that he, along with my Aunt/ Mum Diana, brought me and my brother Darren up after our biological mum Pat died.

When I started the challenge, I never thought I would do so well, but now I was close to the top of the leader board and I wanted to come 1st for Des.

I figured if I ran until 3.30am I would hit the top of the leader board, so I kept on going. After an hour of running, it was the moment of truth. I stopped and went to upload my miles to see if I was 1st. I was thinking this could be it; this could be my moment of glory! But as I looked at my phone, I stood there in disbelief as my GPS hadn't picked up the miles. I had been running for an hour for nothing, I couldn't believe it. I was still in 3rd place and it was now 3.30am. At that point I could have given up and settled for 3rd, but people who win in the game of life don't give in when they know they have more to give. There was no certainty that my GPS would work, but I went for it again and ran until 4.30am. I took my phone out of my pocket, synchronised the miles, and this time it worked. I was now 1st out of over 40,000 people.

I went into the hospital and told Des that I'd been doing a running challenge. I told him that I was trying to get to the top for him, but I was having a challenge with my GPS and a Scottish guy who was in 1st place, so it didn't look likely I was going to beat him. As he lay there looking at me with a tube down his throat I said, "But I carried on and managed to knock that Scottish bastard off the top."

He was clearly in a lot of pain, but he laughed, and I could see he was proud of me.

It was the last time I would see him laugh, as he passed away several weeks later.

After that first day, I thought all the top runners would put more miles in than I could do and I would be knocked out of the top 10, but it never happened. I consistently hit the top of the leader board for the next week until I picked up an injury and couldn't run any more.

I took the next 3 weeks off with the injury, and one day before the next challenge my injury was healed. I thought to myself, "I've had 3 weeks without any training, so it isn't realistic I'll come 1st again," as I always lose a lot of fitness when I have more than a few days off training. My goal this time was to come in the top 10. If I could come 8th, 9th, or 10th, I would be over the moon, but it never happened. I hit 1st place on the 1st day and consistently came 1st until my synchronisation broke down (the app stopped working for some reason) after a week of running. After 7 days, I was 23 miles ahead of my nearest rival in 2nd place and this time I was 1st out of 51,000 runners.

This is what I love about doing well in endurance: you have to earn it. There are certain things in this world that you can get by luck, like a slim physique, good looks, or money (if someone just gives it to you for nothing). But when it comes to achieving in the world of fitness, you have to graft for it. You've got to put the effort in, and you've got to push yourself both mentally and physically.

The main purpose of this story is to show you that:

1. You need a goal.

2. You need to put the effort in.

3. You need to persist when things are uncomfortable and when things go wrong.

# CHAPTER 13

# RUNNERS – THE BEST OF THE BEST

*"The first race I ran, I fell."*
– Usain Bolt

# The Underdog

While I have done OK with running, there are people who have far surpassed my running achievements. Hang on a minute. If I'm writing a book to inspire people based on some of my achievements, should I really shout out about what great things others have achieved? After all, they may make my running achievements look tiny in comparison.

Having that thought process itself is a big achievement. Having the ability to let go of your ego to an extent is a good thing, because when you do that you see the bigger picture. You see that you are not the master of the universe and you are operating on a higher level of consciousness than maybe you were a few years ago.

Compared to the size of the universe, we as individuals are like a grain of sand on a beach.

So before we get all high and mighty because we have achieved one or two things, we need to also realise that whatever level we get to in this world, we are still tiny, tiny, fish in a very, very big pond.

Yes, even if you are a Prime Minister, King or President of a country or you are at the top of your game, it is still all small stuff in the grand scheme of things. That being said, each and every one of us is special and can make a positive difference in not only our own lives but also in the lives of other people.

When I started looking at people who have done ultra-running (running beyond a marathon) I decided to check out the main people in this sport. After a little bit of research, I came across a man who stood apart from everyone else. To put into perspective how good he is, he is the only runner to my knowledge that has been accused of cheating and the cheating accusation has eventually become a badge of honour. He was that good and that far ahead of everyone else, at his first official ultra-distance run, the officials thought it was simply impossible for a human to run that far and that fast in such a short time frame.

In 1983, a group of super-fit ultra-distance runners turned up for the first Spartathlon. Let us not get this confused with the Spartan Race. The Spartan races can be tough depending on how fast you want to run, and they're anything from 3 miles with obstacles to 26 miles with obstacles. These are great races, along with many other races that are popping up all over the world.

However, the Spartathlon is a completely different animal!

In order to even qualify for the Spartathlon you either have to:

- Run 100k (62 miles) in less than 10 hours 30 minutes; or

- Complete a 200km (120 miles) race in under 29 hours and 30 minutes.

The Spartathlon is a 246km (153 miles) beast of a race held annually in Greece, where the runners run from Athens to Sparta. Yes, that's right, if you have seen it, it's that place from the movie 300 where King Leonidas (played by Gerard Butler) shouts, "THIS IS SPARTA!" and kicks a rather rude person into a big pit.

I guess the moral of the story there is, don't go around threatening people and then stand in front of a very deep pit.

Anyway, this unknown runner rocks up to the Spartathlon and decides to take on a field of established international runners. Some the international runners were record-breakers, so it was assumed that the winner would come from this field of top runners. No one gave much thought to the newbie underdog who had showed up for the first time.

He ended up winning the event and was over two-and-a-half hours ahead of the person who came second. Everyone naturally thought this unknown guy had cut the course and cheated, so the next year he was watched like a hawk at every step by the race officials. The race goes over two mountain ranges with steep hills and rocky tracks. To the amazement of race officials and spectators, it took this man less than 7 hours to hit 100km. He got to the 100-mile point in less than 13 hours and ran the last 50 miles in under 9 hours.

He destroyed every top ultra-runner that took him on, and he broke world records left, right and centre.

In 1997, at the age of 41, he completed what is said by many to be the most phenomenal endurance feat in history. In the space of only 24 hours he ran 188 miles! That is the equivalent of 7 marathons back to back in one day. People sometimes talk about a long-distance runner being slow, but being slow is not a tag I would put on this man. When going for this 24-hour run, he ran the first 100k (62 miles) in 7:15. That's 31 miles in 3 hours 38 minutes. Many people would be happy to complete a 26.2

mile marathon in 3.38 never mind running 31 miles in that time and doing another 157 miles straight after.

In terms of the most phenomenal endurance feat in history, I would argue that there are two other superhuman feats that could challenge that. One man ran 1,000 kilometres (621 miles) in 5 days, 16 hours and 17 minutes. Throughout the 6-day race, he only slept for around 2 hours.

The other crazy feat was man ran a staggering 1,000 miles in in 10 days, 10 hours, 30 minutes, and 36 seconds... unbelievable! But that man is the same man I have just been writing about.

And that Underdog's name is Yiannis Kouros.

Yiannis Kouros holds World Records from 100 miles to 1,000 miles and went on to break over 154 world records. He became the greatest ultra-distance runner of all time.

> *"When other people get tired, they stop. I don't.*
> *I take over my body with my mind. I tell it that it's*
> *not tired, and it listens."*
> – Yiannis Kouros

When it comes to people who have achieved great things with running there is one other man in my humble opinion that blows everyone else away with succeeding on a grand scale for inspiring people. When I wrote the words "one man who blows everyone else away", I hesitated.

Not because I doubted his achievement, but because you could argue that he was still a boy when he achieved what he achieved. He was a young underdog who at the age of only 20 and in spite of tremendously challenging circumstances, got up and created something so outstanding it has never been beaten.

There are many runners that have covered more miles in a day, who have run much faster and who have run longer overall distances. What makes this young man's story so unique is he had cancer. He had one of his legs amputated and decided to run across Canada and raise $1 million, but things got a little bit bigger than that.

He was only 18 years old when he was diagnosed with bone cancer in his right knee. When he was in the hospital on the cancer ward he was affected by seeing children younger than him who had cancer. He said, "You just can't forget it, I couldn't anyway, I had to try and do something about it".

When I watched his story on YouTube, it reminded me of a quote which always stuck with me. The quote was from a deaf and blind lady who was an author, political activist, and lecturer, called Helen Keller. She said:

"I am only one, but still I am one. I cannot do everything, but still I can do something; I will not refuse to do something I can do."

This young man's thinking was in line with Helen Keller's. Even though we cannot sort all of the world's challenges out, we can all do a little bit to make the world a better place.

Before he set out to run across Canada, he trained for 14 months. His mother was concerned that it was too much for him and she wanted him to run a shorter distance, but his dream was bigger than that. He loved and respected his mother, but he knew he was capable of doing more, so he stuck with his dream. Even though some people may want to shrink your dream, ultimately you have to follow your heart and choose your own path.

On 12 April 1980, at the most easterly point of Canada, he began his run, which was called The Marathon of Hope. The goal was to run a marathon every day from coast to coast, which was over 5,000 miles. This would be a great achievement for anyone with two legs and in perfect health, never mind someone who had cancer and was running on a wooden prosthetic leg. He would get up at 4am and start running, no matter what weather he faced outside.

For most of the run he was on his own: it was covered in some local papers, but not many people in Canada knew about it. Some local people would stop and put donations into buckets that his friend and brother held out while they followed behind him in a support vehicle. The road was lonely at times and the donations were very small. It looked very unlikely that he was going to raise $1 million, but he kept on going, he kept on putting the miles in.

Life can be a lot like that, we do the work, we put the effort in and sometimes no one seems to care. And even worse, there are many people who will tell you to give up. They will say or think things like:

- Give up, it is not worth it.

- What is the point in doing that?

- You cannot make a difference.

- You are dreaming.

- You have bitten off more than you can chew.

But high achievers always have these sorts of things said about them. The difference that makes them stand out as a high achiever is that they stick to their dream and keep going.

After two months of running, people started to believe in him and he was invited to a Canadian Football League game. When he entered the stadium, he was announced on the speaker system and all the football fans stood up, clapped, and cheered. This brought his thinking level even higher. Not satisfied with having a goal of raising $1 million, he decided that the goal should be to raise $1 for each Canadian, and back in the 1980s that was 24 million people. Would he raise $24 million? The odds were staggeringly against this underdog. These were the days of no smartphones, no Facebook, no Twitter, no YouTube, and no Internet, or at least not the Web as we know it today.

When he got to Toronto, thousands of people came out to support him, as he had inspired a nation. Things were going well, and he was going from strength to strength, he was putting in the miles, people from all over Canada were supporting him and the donations came flooding in.

He kept on running, but as he got to a place called Thunder Bay, he asked to be taken to hospital as he did not feel well. When the doctors examined him they found that he had big tumours on both sides of his lungs. Several days after that, he was taken to hospital in Vancouver and a fundraising telethon was organised. He had raised over $2 million and the telethon raised over $10 million more. He later told his mother that his biggest regret was that he did not have a single dollar to buy his family a Christmas present, even though he had raised millions for cancer.

He wrote in his journal, "If I die, at least I'll die happy doing what I wanted to do in life."

On 28 June 1981, he sadly passed away. He ran 3,339 miles (5,373 kilometres) across Canada and on the back of that annual runs were launched. They are now in countries all over the world and have raised over $650 million.

They are the world's largest one-day fundraiser for cancer research.

In the end, the young Canadian underdog inspired people all over the world. He created something spectacular. And he won! This amazing man's name was Terry Fox.

*"I want to try the impossible to show that it could be done."*
– Terry Fox

# CHAPTER 14

# WINNERS AND LOSERS

*"There is nothing noble in being superior to your fellow man;*
*true nobility is being superior to your former self."*
– Ernest Hemingway

# The Underdog

If you genuinely want to change your life, then you must change the things you are doing on a day-to-day basis.

Many people want change in their lives but simply do not change anything they are doing to make things better. They sit around and wish for a lucky break. Generally, the so-called lucky break will come after a series of failures, which involve trying something out. If you sincerely want to change things, then you must be willing to change.

It is very easy to look for excuses not to change. Many of us look at people like pop stars or movie stars and say things like, "It is easy for them to stay in shape; they can afford personal trainers". Of course they can afford personal trainers but you, too, can get trained for either a small amount of money or no money.

There may be something you can offer the trainer in return: a product or service that you are expert in. I had one client who was good at certain areas of marketing, so I said, "Rather than you pay me, how about you help me with marketing, and I'll train you?" We swapped an hour of my time for an hour of his time; it was like the old bartering system, and it worked well.

Or you can find a friend that is willing to do some training with you. At first you may struggle to find one of your friends who does fitness training. It's easy to rationalise it and say, "I can't find anyone to train with" and give up. You have to move into a different group of people, I am not saying you have to leave all your friends and never communicate with them, I am saying to be a success at something you need to find someone who is already successful at what you want to succeed in. I cannot emphasise this point enough.

Being around that person will motivate you to achieve things you have never achieved before.

I recently saw a trainer on YouTube who was raising his voice and calling people a fucking loser if they had not achieved certain things with their lives. Some people respond to this sort of talk well, and for others it makes them feel like crap. But no one on this Earth is a loser: we all have an important role to play in this world, and everyone's actions will send out a ripple in the pond of life. You can send out positive, loving, encouraging messages or negative, criticising, hateful messages. What sort of ripple we send out is up to us. Just remember that the boomerang you send out will be in the boomerang you get back. Of course, you can be nicest, happiest, friendliest, most loving person in the world and life can still bring you to your knees. We will all go through tough times, but the nicer and more giving we are, the more likely it is that life will bring us the same in return.

Sometimes people say negative things because the other person may have hurt them in some way, but if you are going around calling people a loser because you have achieved more than them, maybe you need to practise some humility. We all start from somewhere and we all have our own personal journeys. If you are making progress in an important area of your life, then you are a winner, and if you have hit a roadblock and are not progressing, then maybe it is time to take a step back and assess the situation. It could be you need to take a different approach or it maybe you just need to persist more.

If you think "I am a winner and you are a loser," maybe it's time to read some books like the "Tao de Ching" or read some Jesus and Buddha quotes. How many times did you hear or read about people like Jesus, Buddha and other great people saying, "You're a loser?"

As I am writing this I am literally laughing, because it is

crazy to think that was the sort of thing they were teaching.

The truth is, you and I are no better than someone else as a human being just because we may have come first in a high-level fitness competition or have more money or have a high level of status because of what we have achieved. There is nothing wrong with having these things, and yes, it is probably better to be super-fit and healthy than to not, and it is probably better to have a lot of money in your pocket than not. But just because someone has a big belly or a low-paid job, it does not make them a loser. You will be able to learn something from each individual on this planet. You may not agree with them, but you can always learn something.

# CHAPTER 15

# PERCEPTION

*"No problem can be solved from the same level of consciousness that created it."*
– Albert Einstein

# The Underdog

One of the greatest movies ever made that covers perception has to be The Matrix. Just in case you haven't seen it, the character Neo is in his little bubble world and is told to believe certain things by the men in suits. I would love to go deeper into this film, but for the purpose of this book I won't. To cut a long story short, Neo unplugs from the system and reaches his full potential.

The system you are plugged into will affect your life, for better or for worse.

Many times, people watch the news and are fearful for their lives because of some danger out there in the world. Sometimes the news can be of great use to us. An example of this would be news of a hurricane that is about to hit where we live. With this sort of warning, we can batten down the hatches or head out of town until the storm has passed. But all too often negative things are reported in the news which builds a climate of fear, terrorist attacks being one of them.

I remember talking to a guy who refused to go to London because he believed that he may get killed in a terrorist attack. He had watched so much negative media it got to the stage where it controlled his life.

Of course it's possible he could get killed, but let's look at some facts to see what the chances are

According to Global Research:

- You are 271 times more likely to die in a workplace accident

- You are 1,904 times more likely to die in a car accident

- You are 33,842 times more likely to die from cancer

- You are 35,079 times more likely to die from heart disease

- You are more likely to die from being struck by lightning than being killed in a terrorist attack.

Since 9/11 about 24 people have died from terrorism in the United States: at the same time more than 100,000 people have been killed in gun-related crime and over 400,000 people have been killed in motor vehicle accidents.

Like many people in the UK, I don't have a religion, however I do believe in a higher power. Whether you have a religion or not doesn't make a difference to me, as I see people as people. But I thought it would be interesting to look at some facts about the religion that is arguably the most vilified religion in the western world.

According to the Huffington Post, the FBI conducted a survey and found that 94% of terrorist attacks in the United States have been by non-Muslims. This means that an American terrorist suspect is over 9 times more likely to be a non-Muslim than a Muslim. In 2010–2015, there were over one thousand terrorist attacks in Europe: what percentage of these attacks were by Muslims? If you're living in the UK or another country that has media and government who are a little on the anti-Muslim side, then the chances are you would believe that at least 80% of those 1,000 + attacks are by Muslims. However the reality is quite different, it's less than 2%. A study was carried out by the University of North Carolina, which showed that fewer than 0.0002% of Americans killed since 9/11 were killed by Muslims.

In 'The Week', it has been reported that there are 1.6 billion Muslims and close to 1.6 billion Muslims have not committed an act of terror.

WHAT IS A TERRORIST?

According to the FBI official website, there is no single, universally accepted definition of terrorism. Terrorism is defined in the Code of Federal Regulations as "the unlawful use of force and violence against persons or property to intimidate or coerce a government, the civilian population, or any segment thereof, in furtherance of political or social objectives".

If you ask many people in the UK if the British are terrorists, of course they will say no. But if we were to look at the past activities of the British within the definition given earlier, then Great Britain doesn't come out squeaky clean here. The British Empire was the biggest empire by land mass in history, and it didn't become that way by asking another country if it could simply take over their country.

I was watching a James Bond movie once where 007 had a meeting with a guy. As they were talking, the man said, "One man's terrorist is another man's freedom fighter."

This made me think about how everything boils down to perception. It's about the environment you're in and what you choose to believe. Many people in Northern Ireland believed the IRA were freedom fighters wanting to get rid of oppressive British rule, but to most people in Great Britain the IRA were terrorists who would all ruthlessly murder innocent people and British soldiers.

So, a lot of conditioning is done from governments and media and many people will believe them. It's brainwashing on a national or even a global scale. It's mainly to do with the people being in charge having more of an influence than the average person. Many of these leaders are influential, they have a belief about something, (even though they could change that belief in the future), and they will push their belief onto other people, even if the facts are wrong. An obvious example of this is the Iraq war.

Don't get me wrong here: I'm not having a political rant or pointing the finger. It is not my place to judge and of course I love being British, but the purpose here is simply to show how people are conditioned and everything is down to perception.

Most people will not let go of certain conditioning, as this can lead to admitting that they were wrong about something, and none of us want to be wrong. None of us want our ego damaged and have to admit that we are not as clever as we thought we were. With this part of the book, you may need to keep an open mind. There are even some people who have been conditioned so strongly that they may reject what is said here, but there is nothing wrong with that.

Part of having a great state of mental health is having the

ability to flow with things, rather than get all bent out of shape and angry. It's far better to be like water, where you can flow around things and gradually wear the situation away over time. But there are also times when you have to stand firm like a rock in certain situations.

There are many ways to solve challenges, and in the end only you can decide how to handle those challenges. Every single human being on this planet is a product of what they have fed their minds or what they have been fed by different sources. We may all think that we are too clever to be led by other people, but we are all influenced by certain things.

Here is a question you could ask yourself: "Have you ever had a belief about something that you later found out wasn't true?" I know I have.

This was highlighted to me while writing this book. Léon's tooth was wobbling, and it looked like he was about to lose his first tooth. While on the phone one day to his mum, she mentioned that this would be the first tooth he would lose. As it was my weekend with him, there needed to be a plan in place where if his tooth came out, I would have to put a £2 coin under his pillow from the tooth fairy. I didn't have to do it, but this wasn't a big deal and so I went along with it.

Was a tooth fairy going to leave a £2 coin under Léon's pillow? As adults we all know the answer to that (at least I hope we all do), but children all over the world are convinced that a tooth fairy exists, and I know I did at one time, like many of us.

How many of us believed that Santa Claus was real at one point in our lives? If you are from many of the western world countries and are a certain religion, then you will probably say you did believe. If you're from a certain isolated tribe deep in the Amazon jungle, then you wouldn't have believed in the Tooth Fairly or Father Christmas. If they knew that you used to believe that an elderly overweight man would climb down your chimney on 25 December every year, while delivering over a billion toys worldwide by means of flying reindeer, I'm sure many of them would think that you've lost the plot.

There are few, if any tribes that haven't been discovered, but I'm sure that if you walked into their tribe with a phone, and a microwave oven (because that's the kind of thing you'd always carry in the jungle) there would be a look of shock on their face. Saying that, when I was on jungle warfare training, I think I would have had a look of shock on my face if someone walked into our camp carrying a microwave oven. You'd be like, "What the fuck?!"

Does that mean you are smarter than them because you know more about technology? No. Does it make them smarter than you for not being fooled into believing in Father Christmas? No. It just means that you have been exposed to different things.

Of course there are people that will say, "Yes, but I was only a child back then," but people can be fooled at any stage of their lives.

Several years ago, I did a 6 month United Nations peacekeeping tour with 29 Commando. One day a riot broke out. At one point I saw a Greek man launch a stone towards the Turks, but the stone hit another Greek man on the back of the head. The man who was hit held his head as the blood poured out of it. Later that evening, I was watching TV. I saw the same incident that I'd witnessed that day being covered on TV. I saw a Turk throw a stone; next I saw the same Greek man that I had seen before holding his head with the blood pouring out of it. I immediately thought that it just didn't happen that way. The Greek man hit the Greek man, but the media edited it to make people believe what the media wanted them to believe. This was the first time I saw how the authorities control how people think and how media can shift people's perceptions.

So before you decide to take on a belief, decide if that

belief will help you and, as Einstein said, "the important thing is not to stop questioning."

# The Underdog

# CHAPTER 16

# THINK FOR YOURSELF

*"Thinking is the hardest work there is, which is probably the reason why so few engage in it."*
– Henry Ford

If you want to achieve big things in life, then you can't be like the majority of people. There is nothing wrong with being average, and if you achieve more than the average person it doesn't necessarily make you a better person. What it can do, though, is give you a sense of pride, and by achieving your goals you might inspire other people, too.

I was talking to my friend Jack Woods one day about how people generally follow the crowd and feel comfortable with that. He referred to most people as "sheeple". At the time I hadn't heard of that expression, but I immediately knew what it meant. Many people follow each other like sheep and have a hard time thinking for themselves. It made me laugh, but I did think it was a good expression.

I was coming over a toll bridge one day and noticed that there were four cars in a queue in one of the lanes. The lane had a green light above the toll which meant it was one of the lanes you could use to get through the toll. I noticed that there was a green light above the lane next to it, but no one was using it. Although people could use the lane, no one was. The reason... they were following the crowd. I passed all the cars that were lined up and went straight to the front of the empty lane, paid my toll, and went through the barrier.

On another occasion, I was out running one morning and was approaching a set of traffic lights. I noticed as I was approaching there was a man standing there waiting for the traffic lights to change to green so he could walk across the road. I noticed that there was no danger from getting hit by a car, so I simply ran across the road.

Waiting for the traffic lights to change to green is often good practice because of safety issues, but there are times when you have to break the rules, go against the norm, and make a decision for yourself. Many people live in fear and never achieve their dreams because they are afraid to think for themselves. They are afraid that they'll get told off by the authorities or that other people will criticise them. If you want to achieve big things, you've got to take chances and take risks. I'm not saying you should get a new career as a cat burglar, but I am saying if you want to live an exciting life you need to have the courage to go after your dreams. On your journey you will stumble, you will fall, you will get knocked back and you will fail at certain points, but you can pick yourself back up and drive through to success!

A similar thing happened when I was in London, walking through the bus station to catch my bus back to Pembrokeshire. A fleet of buses were heading out of the station onto the road. At one point, several of the buses couldn't get out of the station and had to wait for the traffic on the road to clear. One bus stopped directly in front of where I wanted to go so we all stopped and waited for the bus to move out of our way. After about five seconds, I realised that no one knew when the bus would get out of the station, so I decided to walk around the back of the bus and carry on towards my destination.

And guess what happened when I walked around the bus? A load of other people followed me.

These are very simple stories that can happen in everyday life, but the simple point is that many times we need to be the one that makes the move; we need to be the one that takes that first step. Just because an obstacle has been put in our way, it doesn't mean that it's the end of the road for us when it comes to reaching our goals.

At some point in your life there will be a time where you have no experience with what you want to achieve, but if your dream is big enough, you will find a way.

Sometimes the traffic lights are on red, telling you that now is not the time, but sometimes you can't wait for all the signs to say "Go!"

Sometimes you have to give yourself that green light and make the move.

# CHAPTER 17

# NOT EVERYONE WILL UNDERSTAND YOUR IDEA

*"All our dreams can come true if we have the courage to pursue them."*
– Walt Disney

# The Underdog

You may have a vision for something that is totally original and outrageous, and you're sure it will work. The more original and outrageous your idea is, the harder it can be to convince people it's a good idea.

I consider myself to be a pretty open-minded person, but if someone came up to me in 1998 and said they were going to create a cartoon with the storyline of a pants-wearing sponge living in an underwater city called Bikini Bottom and said it'd be a huge hit one day, I would have thought this person was a little crazy. When I say crazy, I mean it in a good way, because if someone said that to me, it would definitely bring a smile to my face, but at the same time, I would wish them all the best with it.

Just because I can't see someone's vision, it doesn't mean that person's vision will never materialise. We all have our opinions on things, but as wise as we think we are, the truth is, our knowledge is limited.

I was sitting down with Léon one day when Sponge Bob Square Pants came on the TV. After watching a bit of it I was in disbelief at how successful the cartoon has become, which lead me to do some research on how it started and exactly how successful it now is.

Sponge Bob Square Pants was created by a marine biologist called Stephen Hillenburg, and like Walt Disney, Hillenburg liked to draw.

Many people reading this book may already know that the Sponge Bob character is very energetic and optimistic, which are two keys to reaching your goals, even if you aren't a sponge.

Before Hillenburg created Sponge Bob, he created another animation called The Intertidal Zone, which taught students about the life of animals in tide pools. He tried to get his comic published but was turned down by everyone he sent the comic to.

He then made an animation film called Wormholes, which was about the theory of relativity, and he met Joe Murray, who was the creator of a popular Nickelodeon animated series. Murray offered Hillenburg a job, Hillenburg got his foot in the door with Nickelodeon, created a character out of one of the strangest sea creatures, and the rest is history.

Stephen Hillenburg's Sponge Bob Square Pants went on to win 12 Kids' Choice Awards, 8 Golden Reel Awards, 6 Annie Awards, 2 Emmy Awards and 2 BAFTA Awards. It is the most distributed property of MTV and the highest-rated series in Nickelodeon's history, and the media franchise has generated a staggering $8 billion. Stephen Hillenburg now does what he loves doing and has pocketed over $90 million in the process.

Even though I don't get the whole Sponge Bob thing, I love the story of how it was made and there is no denying that Stephen Hillenburg and his team have gone on to create something very special that many children (and some adults) love.

Here are some of the key principles that Stephen Hillenburg used to succeed. They are also the keys to success in running, sports, public speaking, business, the arts, or anything else:

1.  Have a vision.

2.  Do something you are passionate about.

3.  Start small and build up to greater things.

4.  Create a product or brand.

5. Get your foot in the door with the right people and organisations.

6. Learn from the people who have done the type of thing that you want to do.

7. Never give in, even if you get rejected by lots of people.

# CHAPTER 18

# SEIZING THE DAY

*"Learn from yesterday, live for today, hope for tomorrow."*
– Albert Einstein

# The Underdog

Many people have this thing where they want to save all their money for a rainy day. There is nothing wrong with that, but what is crazy is working all the time and never having any fun time. By all means work hard, but if you don't reward yourself along the way, then what's it all for? A few years ago I was a support worker where I would take people out who had certain challenges (epilepsy, brain injury, learning difficulties, etc.). I had been taking a gentleman in his early 50s who was challenged with epilepsy for several years, and I was on my way to his house to take him out for a few hours. As always, I arrived at his dad's house where he lived, knocked on the door and waited for the door to be opened. After a few minutes, his dad opened the door. I went into the usual routine and asked whether my client (his son) was ready to go out for a few hours, to which his dad replied, "He's not here". There was nothing unusual about this, as my client often went for a walk on his own, and I usually had to go and find him.

"When will he be back?" I asked. His dad said, "He's gone".

"Gone where?" The answer from his dad took me aback, as it wasn't something I expected to hear: "He's dead". Complete silence. It was like one of those scenes you see on TV where tumbleweed blows past you in the wind.

It turned out that he had died in the night. I couldn't help feeling for his poor dad who had only just lost his wife a year or two before and now his son was gone.

One of the things that I thought about was how my client loved Elvis and how he had always dreamed about going to Graceland for a once-in-a-lifetime trip. He had the money in his bank account to make the trip a reality and I encouraged him to take the trip, but sadly he never did. His dream of seeing the King of Rock-and-Roll's house died with him. It was something I'll never forget, and it made me think that we should seize the day when we can, because we never know what's around the corner.

# CHAPTER 19

# TAKING OPPORTUNITIES

*"When one door closes another door opens; but we so often look so long and so regretfully upon the closed door, that we do not see the ones which open for us."*
– Alexander Graham Bell

# The Underdog

In 2015, I was asked to do security at a military camp. The question I was asked was, "Would you like to do some security work at a military camp?" My answer was, "No, not really." But after I'd said that, I felt that I needed to know where the camp was and asked. The answer that came back was, "It's in a place called Trecwn." This immediately got my interest up. In Pembrokeshire, Trecwn is well-known to some people as a kind of an Area 51 place. It has always been out of bounds to the public as far as I was aware, and all I knew about it was that it was used as a military base in World War 2 where it stored ammunition, but I wasn't even sure of that. I was 90% convinced that I wanted to go there just to have a look around, but I asked a second question: "What's happening there?" The answer came back, "I'm not supposed to say anything about it, but some ex-Special Forces guys are doing some sort of TV show there. That was it... I was sold! I didn't even care about being paid, I just wanted to get into this mysterious place and meet the ex SF lads.

I ended up doing the security on the camp for the TV show that was about Special Forces Selection (it was later released on Channel 4 as SAS Who Dares Wins).

I met some of the lads who were ex-Special Forces and we had a chat about what we were doing now and in the future.

It was great talking to the SBS (Special Boat Service) guys who had done the same sort of course as me in the forces. As we chatted, I told Ollie and Foxy that I had a lot of respect for what they'd achieved. I remember saying, "Fair play, guys, you took it to the next level with going for the SBS after the Commando Course."

They were gracious and humble about the compliment, and I admired that about them. Do you have to be gracious and humble to be successful? You only have to look at Muhammad Ali or Donald Trump to know the answer to that question. So you can be successful by having a different personality to other successful people.

Although I never had an interest in going into the SAS or SBS, I've always had lots of respect for them for passing such a tough course. Out of every 100 people that go for the course, only 10% (or fewer) make the grade.

I showed them some of the things I'd done since leaving

the forces and as I was walking off, Ollie turned to me and said, "Seriously, mate, that's really impressive, what you've achieved!"

People that know me well know that I don't really crave praise, but I have to say that Ollie's comment really made me stop and think. I have a lot of respect for what Ollie's achieved by passing the Commando Course, SAS Selection and the SBS Course, and I was extremely grateful that someone from a unit that I respected so much would say something so nice to me. I can honestly say I had a "moment."

It made me think back to when I had little confidence and was bullied, and when I thought I was destined to achieve very little in life.

Sometimes it's difficult to believe you will achieve big things, I certainly would never have believed that I would have achieved the things I have done. But it all starts with having a goal, taking action, and grabbing opportunities with both hands.

If you're overweight and you want to get fitter and slimmer, great. The chances are you have two legs, so you have a great opportunity to go for a run or go out cycling.

If you want to build a better body for yourself, great. The

chances are you've got a set of arms, so you have a great opportunity to do some push-ups or pull-ups or lift some weights and change yourself.

I interviewed former Royal Marines Mark Ormrod and Joe Townsend, who lost limbs whilst serving in Afghanistan. Both Mark and Joe are doing great things in the world of fitness. Yes, they both lost their legs (Mark also lost an arm), but they decided that there was still an opportunity for them to achieve great things. They took their lives to the next level and inspire people from all over the world.

# CHAPTER 20

# BEING A DIAMOND

*"A diamond starts out rough and unpolished. But with enough pressure and in the right hands, it becomes tough and shines, and so can you."*

– Mark Llewhellin

# The Underdog

There are very few things that will be as important to you as building mental toughness. This is something that I talk about several times throughout this book, simply because it is one of the most important things you can do in life. You can be born into a life with great parents, you can have great genetics, a great physique, lots of money, great looks and every advantage that can be given to you, but if you do not develop mental toughness, life will chew you up and spit you out! The tougher you are mentally, the easier you will find things when life sends its inevitable challenges your way.

- A diamond is made from carbon, the same element that makes graphite and coal.

- Diamond is the hardest material known to man because of the way it has bonded together.

- Both graphite and diamond are made from carbon, but their structures are very different.

It is the same with people: we are all made from the same stuff (carbon also being one of the elements), but we are not all the same when it comes to how much we achieve and how strong we are mentally. People who achieve highly in life bond certain habits and certain principles together that leads to success.

The difference between graphite and diamond is very subtle, but there is a difference. With the habits we use in our daily life, that tiny difference makes a world of difference in the end. When we see people walking down the street, they all pretty much look the same on the outside. Yes, of course there are differences, but most of us have ears, mouths, noses, eyes, arms, and legs, etc. But what we cannot see is what's going on internally in our brains and how things are bonded together.

Experts believe that diamonds are created at roughly 100 miles below the Earth's surface and can take millions or billions of years to form. Like the diamond, it takes time for us to mature and develop into something brilliant. You don't get super-fit by having the odd run. You become super-fit from years of practice. And it's the same with any craft; it takes time, patience and relentless persistence to shine.

Diamonds are formed deep in the Earth's mantle, which is the layer between the Earth's crust and the extremely hot core. Down there it changes the molecular structure of carbon by crushing the atoms together and forcing them into a new structure, making it extremely tough. Under extreme pressure and temperatures carbon becomes diamond, and the diamond gets to the surface through rare, violent volcanic eruptions, which are then blasted to the surface in a host rock called kimberlite.

Like the diamond deep in the Earth, we will also go through challenging times and face extreme pressures and dark moments when we may feel there is no way out.

As the kimberlite transports the diamond, we can also use transporters to help us through to the surface and the light.

These transporters can come in several different forms. They can come in the form of reading self-development books, listening to inspirational people or through friends and family helping us. No matter how tough you are, there will be times when you need outside support. As the old saying goes, no man is an island.

Diamonds occur naturally in the Earth, but getting the diamond out of the Earth is very tough. For every 1 carat of diamond you have to move approximately 200 tons of rock.

Having a high level of mental toughness and success requires digging deep, and the higher you go in life, the deeper you will have to dig.

Characters are formed through challenging circumstances. Every one of us will face challenges in life whether it be moral, financial, physical, or mental. Challenges are just a part of life that we have to accept, and we can either rise to the challenge or crumble and give up. The choice is ours!

Yes, the choice really is yours; you will be the one that decides how you are going to react to a certain situation. You can think your situation is hopeless and you will never get out of it, or you can decide that you are too strong for anything to destroy you mentally. Of course, this is easier said than done but, you are stronger than any situation that will ever get thrown at you.

So if you're looking to take your life to the next level, be prepared to go through some dark times and get crushed and put under extreme pressure. And by following many of the principles in this book, you will come out like a diamond, tough and shining for all to see.

*"When you are inspired by some great purpose, some extraordinary project, all your thoughts break their bonds: Your mind transcends limitations, your consciousness expands in every direction, and you find yourself in a new, great and wonderful world. Dormant forces, faculties and talents become alive, and you discover yourself to be a greater person by far than you ever dreamed yourself to be."*

**– Patañjali**

# ACKNOWLEDGEMENTS

It's almost impossible to say how many people have helped me along the way with producing this book, and if you're not in the acknowledgements just know that I am very grateful for your support and help.

However, I would like to say a massive THANK YOU to a few people that I can think of, off the top of my head:

Paul 'The Viking' Hughes, Eva Savage, Debbie Richards, Mark 'Billy' Billingham, Julie Colombino-Billingham, Tracy, Kay and Maria Morris, Tom Webb, Ambreen Chunara, Mathew and Nafisa Burden, Lucy Duncombe, Cheryl Hicks, Jamie Baulch, Gene Hipgrave, Kauri-Romet Aadamsoo, Matt Dix, David Poole, Simon Eastop, Mark Dawson, Craig Martelle, Michael Anderle, Sat Sanghera, Michael and Emma Byrne, Paul 'Faz' Farrington, James Atkinson and Laura Taylor.

Also, a huge THANKS to 'The Mark Llewhellin Advance Reader Team' for taking the time to read the manuscript and make suggestions.

Live Your Dreams!

Mark

# ABOUT THE AUTHOR

In 1990, Mark Llewhellin left school without knowing his grades. He had little confidence and was not at all optimistic about his future.

Not knowing what to do with his life Mark followed some of his friends into the Army. He failed his basic 1.5-mile run, was bullied, and was also voted the fattest person in the Troop!

After a year with the Junior Leaders Regiment Royal Artillery, Mark decided he would try and get into 29 Commando Regiment Royal Artillery, which is an elite Army Commando Regiment that at the time proudly held the Military Marathon World Record (i.e. a marathon carrying a 40lbs backpack).

After failing the 29 Commando Selection phase (called 'The Beat Up') twice, first through lack of fitness and secondly through an injury, Mark subsequently passed on his third attempt and completed the 'All Arms Commando Course' on his first attempt.

Mark later went on to achieve the following:

- Break the 100-kilometre Treadmill World Record.

- Place 1st in the Strava Distance Challenge in 2015 competing against over 51,000 runners.

- Place 1st in the Strava Distance Challenge in 2014 competing against over 40,000 runners.

- Run and walk 70-miles without training on his 40th birthday.

- Become a successful Personal Fitness Trainer.

- Complete the Marathon Des Sables (a six-day, 135-mile ultra-marathon in the Sahara Desert).

- Work and live in London's exclusive Park Lane as a Bodyguard.

- Run 1,620 miles in the United States whilst carrying a 35lbs pack.

Mark has interviewed some of the world's top performers and high achievers in various locations, including one of the world's most prestigious memorabilia rooms...the Hard Rock Café Vault Room in London.

He has travelled to over 50 countries and has been featured in leading national newspapers and on TV for his running achievements.

Mark has extensively worked in the support and care industry for many years helping individuals with brain injury, autism, epilepsy, dyspraxia, and various types of learning difficulties.

He is the Managing Director of Mark 7 Productions, as well as the Producer and Host of 'An Audience with Mark Billy Billingham' speaking events around the UK.

Mark is currently working on more personal development books and lives with his son Léon (when Léon's not at his Mum's) on a beautiful marina in South West Wales.

# ALSO BY MARK LLEWHELLIN

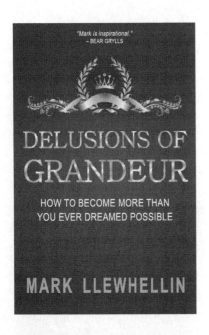

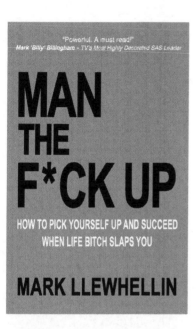

"Powerful. A must read!"
Mark 'Billy' Billingham – TV's Most Highly Decorated SAS Leader

# MAN THE F*CK UP

HOW TO PICK YOURSELF UP AND SUCCEED
WHEN LIFE BITCH SLAPS YOU

## MARK LLEWHELLIN

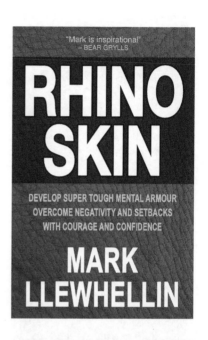

"Mark is inspirational"
– BEAR GRYLLS

# RHINO SKIN

DEVELOP SUPER TOUGH MENTAL ARMOUR
OVERCOME NEGATIVITY AND SETBACKS
WITH COURAGE AND CONFIDENCE

## MARK LLEWHELLIN

NUMBER 1 BESTSELLING AUTHOR

# STAY STRONG

ELIMINATE NEGATIVE THINKING AND BECOME
A STRONGER AND MORE POSITIVE PERSON

## MARK LLEWHELLIN

"POWERFUL!"
Kate Strong – World Triathlon Champion

# PUT YOUR BIG BOY PANTS ON

HOW TO MASTER YOUR MIND AND EMOTIONS
BUILD SUPERIOR MENTAL TOUGHNESS
THINK POSITIVE AND LIVE THE GOOD LIFE

## MARK LLEWHELLIN

Sign up for free at www.markllewhellin.com for offers, updates and new releases.

# DISCLAIMER

Although the author and publisher have made every effort to ensure that the information contained in this book was accurate at the time of release, the author and publisher do not assume and hereby disclaim any liability to any party for any loss, damage, or disruption caused by errors or omissions in this book, whether such errors or omissions result from negligence, accident, or any other cause.

A Mark 7 Publications Paperback.

First published in Great Britain in 2017

by Mark 7 Publications

Copyright © Mark 7 Publications 2017

The moral right of Mark Llewhellin to be identified as the author of this work has been asserted by him in accordance with the Copyright, Designs and Patents Act 1988.

ISBN 978-0-9956501-0-7

Book design and formatting by Tom Webb
pixelfiddler@hotmail.co.uk

# IF YOU ENJOYED THIS BOOK

Your help in spreading the word about Mark's books is greatly appreciated and your reviews make a huge difference to help new readers change their lives for the better.

If you found this book useful please leave a review on the platform you purchased it on.

Printed in Great Britain
by Amazon